# Law School: Get in a Position to WIN!

*A must read if you're thinking about law school, especially part time law school*

ANKIT KAPOOR

Copyright © 2017 Ankit Kapoor
All rights reserved.

ISBN: 1545436800
ISBN 13: 9781545436806

# TABLE OF CONTENTS

| | | |
|---|---|---|
| Acknowledgements | | v |
| Preface | | vii |
| 1 | Hustle | 1 |
| 2 | Know the *WHY?* | 3 |
| 3 | Time | 7 |
| 4 | Scholarship | 10 |
| 5 | Choosing the right school | 13 |
| 6 | Your first year | 15 |
| 7 | Beyond your first year | 21 |
| 8 | Win | 26 |
| 9 | Make Law School Count | 31 |

# ACKNOWLEDGEMENTS

First of all, I want to thank my family for making law school possible for me. Without their support, I would not be in law school and certainly not writing this book. Secondly, I want to thank everyone else who played a part in making my first book possible. From those who helped with editing to those who read it and provided feedback, I appreciate everyone's time and input. Lastly, thank you– the reader. I hope you find this book informative and worthwhile.

# PREFACE

This book is written to help you conquer your next obstacle – getting through law school. It is a short book on purpose. I want you to be able to refer to it throughout your studies and reread it if necessary during your breaks. Another reason I kept it short is because no one who is about to begin or is enrolled in law school wants to spend time reading a 200-page book. The reality is that you do not have the time for additional reading. That is why I designed this book the way I did. The content in it will get you ready for starting law school and will assist you throughout your legal studies.

I highlighted some of the crucial mistakes I made while in school that I want to help you avoid. As the saying goes, "a wise man learns from his mistakes, but a wiser man learns from mistakes of others." Learn from my mistakes. Follow the principles and advice in this book. It is a quick, easy, and helpful read unlike many other books out there detailing how to get through law school. The general principles in this book are very important. This book *will* put you in a position to win in law school. The rest is up to you. There are no guarantees in life so you have to put in the work.

Ankit Kapoor
Brooklyn, New York

# 1

# HUSTLE

*Using strenuous efforts to get closer to where you want to be*

If you bought this book, chances are you are either thinking about attending law school, are going to soon begin law school, are in law school, or are a friend/family member who wanted to support my first book.

Well, if you are in one of the first three categories, I suggest you get acquainted with the word *hustle*. If you are not willing to hustle, I want you to put this book down or turn off your kindle and email me for a full refund (I am serious). In fact, just quit thinking about law school right now. It is not for you.

Now, if you are still reading, chances are I have not offended you and you are still somewhat interested in hearing what I have to say and even pursuing law school. You see, I chose to begin the book in this manner because law school is a hustle. You cannot forget that under any circumstances. The second you do, you will slack off, forget why you began law school, wonder where you went wrong, and why you did not land that $180,000 corporate associate position at a large law firm (also known as "big law").

Yes, I know what you may be thinking. You do not want to land that big law position. Money is not important to you. You do not want to work

80 hours per week (side note: not entirely true). You want to be a public interest lawyer or perhaps you want to open up your own firm soon after finishing law school. That is all perfectly fine, but guess what? You still have to hustle. Why else would you commit five years (half a decade!) between studying for the LSAT, applying to schools, and spending four years, three for full time students, in night classes?

Currently, I am working as a Police Officer at the NYPD and attending Brooklyn Law School as a part-time evening student. You may wonder why I did not just quit being a police officer and go to law school full-time. Those reasons, along with why I became a Police Officer to begin with, are beyond the scope of this book. I chose to write this book because every time I meet someone who is not a part-time law student, and he/she learns that I am a full-time Police Officer and a law student, the common question they ask is, "How do you do it?" Or they make a statement, "I don't know how you do it." This was the inspiration behind this book. I even meet other police officers who are considering law school because they want to transition into a new career or build upon their career in the police department but they don't know where to begin.

Well, in this book, I'm going to answer all those questions truthfully. Let me assure you that I am no anomaly. Every year, thousands of students choose to begin this journey. Heck, some of the hardest working people I know are current evening law students who began law school with me. I just want people to know the reality of law school. As you can probably tell by now, I am not here to sugar coat anything, tell you what you want to hear, or even tell you that law school is not as hard as people say. I am here to tell you that law school is a hustle.

# 2

## KNOW THE *WHY*?

Why do you want to go to law school? Why do you want to become an attorney? For anyone who is thinking about law school or currently enrolled, you have to know your true motivations for becoming an attorney. While law school is certainly an animal of its own, it does not necessarily get easier when you become a practicing attorney. The practice of law is a super saturated, ultra-competitive profession. Lawyers do not work the 9 to 5. The work does not always end in your office. Depending on the kind of law and geographic location, it can require working on a weekend or late nights.

As a matter of fact, if you want to make any real money, it will definitely require working the occasional weekend and the late nights. Hence, you have to be willing to hustle and you have to know your *why*. If money is the sole reason, quit your law school plans now. If you are already in law school and have a substantial amount of credits to complete, drop out now. Stop wasting time and money. Law school will not be your path to riches. Even if you find the riches, chances are you probably will not be happy.

While I cannot answer the "why" questions for you, I will answer why I made this commitment. During my second year as an NYPD police officer, I came to the realization that what I was doing was not too much different from the work of an attorney. Think about it. One day you are having a problem and you need some help. Let us use a common problem most of us have experienced – a minor car accident. You get into a car accident with another motorist. You and the motorist dispute as to who is at fault. Clearly, it is the other guy's fault, but he wants to hold you accountable. You call 911 and the officer(s) arrive. He takes you aside and asks you what happened. You tell him your problem because you need his expertise to resolve the dispute. The officer then advises you that he is going to prepare an accident report and under the law, the other motorist is at fault because he rear-ended you. He may also advise you on how this affects your license, your insurance, and, if you are hurt, he can call you an ambulance.

What just happened there? It is actually very simple. You had a problem, and you wanted the police officer to advise you on how he can be of help. That was part of my underlying rationale for why I decided to become an attorney. Since I interned at a law firm in college, I knew that being an attorney would not be too different. Clients call attorneys because they need help with a situation and need a solution. The attorney advises his/her client on the law, lays out what the client's options are, and informs them how he/she can be of help. I did not see this being too different from what I was already doing. Obviously, I am putting this in very simple terms, but, for our purposes, there is no need to complicate or convolute it.

So, if you are a police officer reading this, you might be a little angry or even wholeheartedly disagree. Perhaps, you are in counter terrorism, and your job entails investigating the next terrorist attack. Maybe you work in the Police Commissioner's office as part of his security detail. You may even be a patrol officer, like I used to be myself, who completely disagrees because lawyers do not make arrests, issue summonses or put their lives on the line every single day. (Do not say that to family law attorneys!) They do not do "God's work" like we do. Yes all of the above is true. However, you all know very well that making arrests and writing summonses is small part of a police officer's daily job. A typical patrol officer who responds to 911 calls is there to advise the caller as to what his or her rights are and to inform the caller as to how he can help.

This is the way I have viewed and still view the legal profession. I decided to attend law school because I saw the correlation between the two careers. I was already familiar with the criminal justice system, the courts, prosecutors and defense lawyers, preparing for and giving courtroom testimony, and other aspects of legal work. Therefore, I figured this would be a fitting transition and I could excel at it. To be frank, I also wanted to make more money. However, money was not my only motivation. It was certainly part of it.

When I first decided to apply to law school, I was working really odd hours and barely had weekends off. So, the irregular schedule and poor quality of life played a part in it. I did not enjoy working those odd hours to then have Tuesday or Wednesday off, or end up doing overtime when I finally have a free weekend to enjoy. Yes, I know it is a sacrifice. Police officers make it every single day throughout the world, but I wanted some stability in my life. I do not see anything wrong with that. It is just a personal preference. This part was not the controlling factor, but definitely had an impact on my decision. While I am aware legal work can also be unpredictable and requires to come in on the occasional weekend or holiday, its other aspects outweighed those considerations.

I admire the fact that lawyers have a direct impact on their clients. This is especially true for those working in small law firms. For example, a police officer has direct impact on a citizen when he responds to a 911 call, a lawyer has a direct impact on a client when he/she helps resolve a legal dispute. Whether it is defending someone who is wrongfully accused or settling a multi-million dollar contract dispute, lawyers take on the responsibility for advocating for their clients. This is something that truly appeals to me about the legal profession.

Thus, I chose to attend law school because it seemed like a natural transition from my being a Police Officer. Additionally, I enjoy problem solving, and I wanted to have the ability to directly impact my client's lives. Lastly, I wanted to make more money doing all of this!

Therefore, before you choose to attend or continue law school, know your true motivations. It cannot be just for money or a career change. You can always make more money elsewhere or change careers. Law school is a hefty time and financial commitment. It is imperative to be there with purpose. Otherwise, you will burn out and will not appreciate all you can learn in law school. After all, how can you hustle towards a goal without a sense of purpose?

# 3

# TIME

*Time is what we want most, but what we use worst.*

So you have figured out a good reason to attend law school. Now you have to figure out whether you have the time. The answer is: yes, you do. Unless you are an investment banker, an Emergency Room doctor, or in another profession that requires you to work 90% of your waking hours, you have the time.

While part-time law school is ideal for a single person, you can do this even if you have a family. Several of my classmates have full-time jobs and families at home. Some even got married, bought a house, and had kids since we started school three years ago. It requires sacrifice. Every hour of the week counts, and you cannot waste it away watching re-runs of Friends or back to back…to back… seasons of Breaking Bad. Do all of that during your winter and summer breaks.

When I started law school, I was working the midnight shift in Bedford Stuyvesant section of Brooklyn. This meant that on most nights I would attend class from 6 PM to 10 PM, get something to eat, and then drive to work. Then from 11 PM to 8 AM I would sit in an NYPD patrol car and answer 911 calls. At the time, I was living with my parents 42 miles away from work. By the time I got home and settled into bed, it was around 10

AM. Then I would sleep until 3:30 in the afternoon, get up, shower, eat and head to law school at 4:30 PM the latest because it would take me at least 90 minutes to get there. Then I would sit in for my 6 PM class and repeat this entire process.

That was my daily routine; not an ideal situation for the first-year law student, but I had to make it work. Then one night, when my partner and I were on our "meal," aka lunch break, I was completing some final edits to my legal memo assignment (in your first year you will have to take a legal writing course and write a legal memo. More on that later). It was around 3 AM, and my partner was in the precinct as I was sitting in the patrol car in the parking lot with my laptop open. One of the precinct unit supervisors observed what I was doing and asked about it. I explained to him that I am in law school and am finishing an assignment. He said he was looking for someone with basic computer skills to add to his unit. These "desk cop" positions are generally frowned upon in the police department, so initially I did not think much about it.

Then I learned that my partner was chosen to be a field-training officer for rookie cops, so I knew I would be without a partner soon. I had already been a floater on patrol. Being a cop with no partner means you are often given assignments that do not require a partner, such as sitting on a hospitalized prisoner or being assigned to a shooting post - a place where a recent shooting took place. At this point in my career being a floater was not something I wanted to revert to. Consequently, I took on that supervisor's offer and became more or less a desk cop. I still go out in the streets occasionally, but this is not even comparable to being a midnight cop in Bedstuy. As I started my second semester in the spring, I went from working midnights to 8 AM to -5 PM with weekends off. As you can probably guess, my quality of life changed drastically and for the better.

It is no secret that law school is a huge time commitment. If you are in the typical four-year evening night law school program, during your first year you will be going to class four nights a week. At least two, sometimes three, of those nights you will be taking back to back classes. For example, one class runs from 6 PM to 8 PM and another from 8 PM to 10 PM. Other nights, you will just have one class. While this may vary from school to school, this is how program is structured at my school and other schools I considered. This is not terrible for those part-time students who do not have a full-time job. For those who have the typical 9 AM to 5 PM job, this is a substantial time commitment.

Law school is not like undergrad. You can't just skim readings and ace the final exam. That one exam will dictate your entire grade in most law school classes. You have to keep up with the reading assignments. Plan on reading close to, if not more than 200 pages per week. Reading is only half the battle. Comprehension is another ball game. You are going to find yourself reading at a pace of 10-15 pages per hour. Therefore, you will need around 15 to 20 hours per week to complete most reading assignments in your first year.

Thus, if you are working 40 hours per week, you have to add at least 10 hours devoted to sitting in class and about another 15 hours reading for those classes. I am not going to go into what kind of things you should be noting or writing as you read – you will learn that during orientation. What I will tell you is that you should plan to commit about 70 hours per week commitment for 13 to 14 weeks per semester for eight semesters. So, ask yourself – do you have the time? I bet you do!

# 4

# SCHOLARSHIP

*When I was young I thought that money is the most important thing in life; now that I am older I know that it is.*

By now you should have figured out whether you have a proper purpose to attend law school and time to commit to it. Now you need the money. If you come from a wealthy family and/or have a 170 or higher LSAT score, you can probably skip this chapter. You probably will not incur much, if any, debt. But for the rest of us, this is a big hurdle.

I think one thing we can agree on is that debt can be crippling for most people. Yes, there is a difference between bad debt (credit cards) and good debt (investment properties), but whether law school is a bad or good debt is entirely up to you. It is a good debt if you are going to law school for the right reasons. It is a bad debt if you are going because you do not know what else to do with your life. Again, you have to be able to answer the *WHY*? Not only because it is a time and money commitment, but you will undoubtedly be asked this question in every single interview during law school and beyond. If you do not have a genuine answer, it will be very hard for you to find a job or enjoy one if you do find it.

Obtaining a scholarship is crucial. Even if you get into Harvard, I would still advise finding some sort of scholarship so that you can rely on student loans as little as possible. Scholarships are offered based on a number of factors such as undergraduate GPA, LSAT score, letters of recommendation, personal statement, etc. In my opinion, your LSAT score is the most important factor. You have to do your research on acceptance scores for the schools you want to attend. Currently, the LSAT is scored from 120 to 180 with 150 being an average score. Let us say that your ideal law school has a median acceptance score of 160. That means you have to score at least 160 or above to be competitive in the scholarship game.

For some reason, your LSAT score can strongly determine how well you will do in law school. At least that is the way law schools see it, and there is some validity to that. A person with a score of 170 who applies to a school with an average acceptance score of 160 will undoubtedly obtain more money in scholarship than the one who scored 160. This is because schools want the 170 students. That student is more likely to do well in law school and be employed after graduation, thereby boosting the school's employment numbers, rankings, and reputation. These are very important statistics to law schools.

This is not to say that if you got a score of 158, you should attend the law school that has an acceptance score of 150. Ideally, you want to be able to attend the highest ranking school that accepted you, but I can tell you that as I approach graduation, it is relieving to know that I do not have a looming $160,000 debt growing with interest waiting for me. I am fortunate enough to be on a decent scholarship and have some help from my parents and a job with the NYPD to help pay the difference.

It is OKAY to go to a lower ranked school. If you are gunning for a part-time program, you will not be able to attend the Ivy League schools anyway since they do not have part-time programs. You will find a job as long as you follow the principles I lay out in the upcoming chapter. It may not be the job you had hoped for right out of school, but a job nonetheless. Yes, a very small percentage of graduates get the higher salaried positions from these schools, but your starting salary out of law school is not that big of a deal. Once you become a more seasoned lawyer, more doors will open up.

Once you get all of your acceptance letters, try to get as much money from the schools as possible. You should leverage one school against the other. For example, if your third choice offered you $50,000 in total scholarship and your first choice offered $25,000, you should write a letter to your first school of choice about why you want to attend it much more than the other one, but the lack of funding is what is holding you back. Some schools do not negotiate, but the odds are you will get them to increase the scholarship close to what other schools are offering.

Out of all the schools I was accepted to, every single one increased their initial offer once I showed them the offering letters from other schools. I even convinced one school to more than double its offer. You can too. You have to be able to negotiate and use leverage. You will see how important this is as you get closer to becoming an attorney. If you do not know how to write a convincing letter getting them to increase their offer, get in touch with me and I will send you the emails I had sent to schools. No need for you to try and reinvent the wheel here.

# 5

# CHOOSING THE RIGHT SCHOOL

Now you know your purpose for attending law school, found the time to do it, and have some money to help pay for it. Great. Next comes choosing the right school for you.

You should have some idea of what kind of law you would like to practice. It would not make sense for you to attend a school with a strong public interest program if your goal is to become a corporate lawyer. Even though I have stressed the importance of scholarship, it really does not make sense to go to a school on scholarship when it does not have a concentration in what you want to learn. Yes, you can change from being a corporate lawyer to a prosecutor or vice-versa, but going in with a clear vision will help avoid confusion where you want to be after law school.

After you have narrowed down your schools, ask the school for their evening class offerings for the last three years. Let's say you want to be an immigration attorney. In your research, you may have discovered your school has a great immigration clinic and a variety of immigration courses. What the course offerings do not show is when those classes are offered. You may find that out of the eight immigration courses your school offers, only one or two are offered in the evenings. Moreover, they may only be offered in alternating years. Even worse, the times may conflict with another class you may want to or have to take.

If you are a current evening student, you understand this struggle. I myself have sat down with students to come up with a proposal for the school's deans so that evening students can have better class options. Look carefully into the course offerings. Sports law sounds like an interesting course, but taking a legal drafting course is probably more useful in practice.

In sum, choose a school that offers classes and clinics in which you are most interested in and then look into previous class offerings to see if they align with what you want to study.

# 6

# YOUR FIRST YEAR

*"First year they scare you, second year they work you,
third year they bore you."*

Congratulations. You figured out your purpose to attend law school, you found the time, you received a good scholarship, and you chose the right school. Now you are going to be (or better be) excited to finally start your first year.

If you know other lawyers, then you have already heard that your first year is your toughest year. I disagree. I think every year is a tough year for part-time evening students. Juggling work, family, and other priorities along with law school can be extremely exhausting. But have no fear – it is manageable. This is also the year when you will make friendships that will last a lifetime.

In your first year of law school. You will be to complete classes in Civil Procedure, Contracts, Torts, Constitutional Law, Criminal Law, Property Law, Legal Writing I and Legal Writing II. The order in which you take those courses varies from school to school, but, in my case, I took Civil Procedure, Torts, and Legal Writing I (11 credits) in the first semester. In my second semester, I took Contracts, Constitutional Law, and Legal Writing II (12credits). Criminal Law was mandatory in the following summer session, and Property Law was offered in the fall of our second year. Full-time students complete these eight classes in their first year.

This means that part-time students take one less class than full-time students during each of their first two semesters. Your 40 hour or more work–week does not equate to an extra class full-time students take, but when it comes to class rank, you will be ranked with your graduating class, including all of the full time students. This is how it is done at my school, and I can't imagine other schools doing it differently.

Class rank matters for three reasons. One is scholarship. Most law school scholarships are contingent upon you maintaining a certain class rank, i.e. top 40% of the class. Second, your resume. This is something highly relied on by employers, at least the top law firms. I'll get into this a bit more in the next chapter. Third, your personal ego and competitive nature. After all, you are not spending all this time and money to lose a scholarship and graduate at the bottom of your class.

Therefore, it is crucial for you to absolutely crush it your first year. I will be honest; I did not. My first year grades were all B's and B+'s. I do not have any excuses, but I am also not sure if I could have worked harder, smarter for sure. Law school finals are no joke, especially first year finals because the classes are anywhere from four to five credits each. So, the final is usually three to four hours long. The legal writing classes are two credits each, but you have writing assignments in lieu of a final exam. The writing classes are probably easier than the other classes, but could be more time consuming throughout the semester.

For your exams, practice, practice, and practice! How? Take the exams from previous years. I barely did this my first year, and my grades obviously reflected that decision. That is surely the best way to prepare for a law school exam. Study with another student or two if you need to. I recommend it. Hearing different perspectives on a particular vague question will help you in your answer. Do not worry about outlining every day/week of the semester as other students would say they do. It is not realistic for part-time students with full-time jobs. Also, you do not have to outline. If you have other methods of studying that work for you, by all means go for it. Do not be pressured into thinking you have to do what everyone else is doing, but, please, take practice exams. Memorizing the law is important, but the application is key.

You will learn more about this in law school, but do not forget to take at least one practice test for each one of your classes. Just do it. If you do not have the time, find it. If you cannot make the time for a full practice exam, outline an answer. Write out the possible arguments and counterarguments in one or two sentences. This is still better than walking into an exam cold. You will learn more about effective test taking strategies in law school, but just heed my advice on taking a practice exam.

A bit on your writing class: In the legal writing class during your first semester, you will learn how to prepare a legal memorandum. This is usually an informative and concise document from an associate (you) to a partner (the professor) discussing possible outcomes of a hypothetical case from a prospective client. You will research on case law, discuss whether the law favors or disfavors your client's case, and deliver it to your professor in a memo format. You will learn the proper formatting and structure in school, but the memo will be around ten to fifteen pages.

For your second semester, you will prepare what is called an appellate brief. Contrary to the informative style of a legal memo, this is an argumentative brief. This will involve a case that is on appeal from the trial court to a higher court – the appellate court. Half of the class will represent the plaintiff while the other half will represent whom? You guessed it–the defendant. You will research case law, outline arguments, and prepare an entire argument advocating whether the appellate court should affirm or reverse the lower court's decision. In addition, you will have to stand in front of your class and advocate for your client in the form of an oral argument. This can be fun or daunting depending on whether you enjoy or dislike public speaking.

Preparing for the oral argument is important not only because it is part of your grade, but also because you will have to participate in Moot Court tryouts using the same argument. Even if you do not want to be a trial lawyer, participation in the tryouts is mandatory. At least it is in my law school. Like a high class rank, employers, especially top law firms, seek students with moot court experience. Whether you get on the moot court depends on a combination of your writing class grade and how well you perform during tryouts.

Finding time to be on Moot Court while taking classes and working full-time is difficult. However, there are usually two divisions, and part-time students get on the division that is less time consuming. Also, you get credit for being on the Moot Court, so you can take one less class or take a two-credit class as opposed to a three-credit one. Considering my B+ in Legal Writing, I did not get on the team. As I have mentioned previously, law school is ultra-competitive.

Your next important goal after attaining spectacular grades your first year is participating in the writing competition for Law Review and other journals. Just as you finish your last final in your first year and think that you are done, you have one more hurdle to climb if you choose to. This is not required, but you should think of it as a requirement. The writing competition determines which journal will give you an offer. Law review and other journals are ranked nationally and within each law school, so it is important to try to join them. The Law Review is the most honorable journal to join. Then there are other journals, such as Journal of International Law, Corporate Law, Public Policy, etc. They vary from school-to-school. Focus on getting on the Law Review or another journal that interests you

Let's focus on the writing competition. The writing competition is basically another paper you will write commenting on a hypothetical case. You will be required to edit footnotes according to this legal citation book called the "Bluebook." You will be required to purchase this book for your legal writing course during your first year. At my school, part-time students had the opportunity to skip the competition their first year and participate in it during the second year. I cannot remember the reason why, but I decided that I would do it at the end of my second year. Just do it while you can. Do not wait until your second year. I skipped it my second year because it was my brother's college graduation that weekend (9 hours away from home). I am not making any excuses, but things happen. Life happens. I screwed up. Learn from my mistakes.

There is another way for you to get on a journal without participating in the writing competition - stellar grades. B's and B+'s will not cut it. If you're in the top 10-15% of your class, you will most likely be invited to the Law Review or another journal. However, I still recommend that you participate in the writing competition and get it over with. It will be worth it, and I will explain in the next chapter why.

Now, there is one thing that I suggest you definitely do not do. This will be obvious to some, but a surprise to others. While many of you are full-time employees and will not have time for such activities, some of you will want to get involved in all these different law school organizations. These organizations vary from school to school, but the idea is that they are similar to clubs or societies in college. You have organizations like the Criminal Law Society, Labor and Employment Law, Asian Lawyers Association, Italian American Law Students, etc. You get the idea. If you really want to join, join just one. It is a great way to meet people and learn more about what your school has to offer.

I joined the Student Bar Association and was elected the class delegate for evening students in my first year. I do not want to say it was a waste of time because I made a couple of good friends, but I think I would have been fine without it. I stepped down after the first year. It was a good conversation piece during interviews, but it was not feasible for someone who works full-time with work schedule similar to mine. I saw some of my friends join multiple organizations, and it is just not worth it. Like everything else in life, it is a time commitment. Yes, you may meet someone whose father is the General Counsel at Amazon. You become best friends with this person, and that is how you get your first law job. It can happen but unlikely nevertheless. Instead of devoting all that time being part of an organization, invest more time towards your classes. You will see a higher return on investment. This advice also applies if you are going to be a full-time student. However, since you will have more free time, join at least one organization. You are allowed to be social.

In sum, your goal is to absolutely crush your first year. You have to go into it with three goals in mind. I will get stellar grades, I will crush the moot court tryouts, and I will get on Law Review or another journal. You know the saying – shoot for the moon because even if you miss, you'll land among the stars. Similar concept. The three goals are the moon for you. If you miss one of them, you will be in a good position even if you reach just two of them.

# 7

# BEYOND YOUR FIRST YEAR

*Hustle*

Congratulations! You have made it past arguably the toughest year of law school. Before I get into this chapter I'd like to make a comment.

Whether or not you did well your first year, got on moot court, on Law Review or another journal, or maintained that scholarship, if you did not enjoy what you have learned or what law school has to offer, I would seriously reevaluate whether law school is the right choice for you. Listen to me very carefully. Do not waste another two to three years of your life doing something you do not enjoy. "Well, I am not sure what else to do with my life, and a law degree is a great credential to have" is NOT a valid reason to stay. Sure, a law degree is a great credential, but if it is not something you are passionate about, you are wasting your time and money. You have already sunk $50,000-60,000. Do not continue and sink another $100,000. It does not matter if you are on a full scholarship because you should factor in the opportunity cost. You can spend that time learning or doing something else. Also, the funds given to you can be better used for someone who actually enjoys law school. While I use the word "enjoy" loosely, many students want to be in law school and can use those funds.

I have met countless people in law school who say they do not even want to be lawyers any more. Most of these students in their second year. Then I wonder, why are you still here? To waste more time and money? If I had to guess, it is the stigma of dropping out that holds them back. The fear of perception of failure. Or they just do not know what else to do with their life. Nevertheless, you should think long and hard about continuing law school if you do not have the passion for it. Oftentimes, we try things and realize it is not what we thought it would be. This is totally normal. There is nothing wrong with feeling that way about law school or anything else you decide to do. Just stop doing that thing.

If you have decided to stay, let us get into what is beyond your first year. Now you can actually choose your classes. You should have an idea of available class options based on your research when choosing the right school and looking at the course offerings. Choose strategically. Do not let this be a liberal arts law degree. Try to specialize in two areas. I know class options are limited for evening students, but try to be consistent. For example, if you want to be in litigation, take Evidence, Trial Advocacy, Discovery, Litigations Skills, etc. If corporate law appeals to you, take Corporations, Corporate Finance, Secured Transactions, Securities Regulation, etc. You get the idea. Try to be consistent and build upon an area of law or two that interest you.

Next comes the hard part. Internships, Externships, and Clinics. Aside from the fact that many law schools have made fieldwork a requirement for graduation, it is crucial that you work at a law firm, clinic, and/or a government organization.

I have participated in four internships throughout my second and third year. I did this while working full-time. People often wonder how this is possible with work and school. Well, for one, I do not have a family yet. I do not have the obligations of a mortgage, wife, kids, or other responsibilities similar to having a family. Second, I am in a unique position at my job where my schedule is slightly flexible to accommodate externships.

During my second year, I had looked at my resume in order to figure out what I had to offer. I was not in the top of the class, I was not on the Moot Court, and I was not on Law Review or a Journal. I took full responsibility for all of those setbacks. I figured there has to be another way I can stand out, and practical experience is something most employers value. As a result, I began applying for various internships. Every place I interviewed at asked me the same question: how will you intern here for twelve to fifteen hours a week and, at the same time, work full-time and go to night classes?

I had to get creative, and I still do. You will also have to get creative. At the time, I was working Monday through Friday. There was a person in my unit who was moving on to another unit, and his work week was from Sunday through Thursday. I figured that this was a perfect opportunity to take his spot and switch my days off so I can at least intern one full day on Friday. That is exactly what I did. In addition, I was fortunate enough to work the afternoon shift on Thursdays so I could devote additional four hours to internships on Thursday mornings from 9 AM to 1 PM. Then I would go to my regular work from 2 PM to 10 PM. Internships will only give you three to four credits, and most semesters you will have to carry a total of eight to ten. So, you will still need to take classes. This was a lot. It is still a lot, but hard work is always rewarded.

Listen. I know this is a bit unrealistic in most office jobs or any job for that matter. NYPD is an organization that never closes, so schedules can be more flexible than other employers might be able to offer. Since that time, I have had the same schedule and interned for four straight semesters.

You may ask why? Here, I am working about fifty hours per week, interning for additional twelve to fifteen hours, and still attending class for four hours a night at least twice per week. It is a lot to have on your plate. However, the experience is worth it; one hundred percent.

There are many reasons for participating in internships/externships during law school. First of all, as I mentioned earlier, fieldwork is required in most schools now. Second, you gain actual practical experience. There is only so much you can learn in a classroom. Some of your professors have not worked at a law firm in decades. They can (in fact, they will) be out of touch with the real life practice. Unless you have worked at a law firm or in some legal capacity elsewhere before, getting this experience is important.

Internships will allow you to learn what you like and dislike in practice. You will also have an opportunity to network, work on actual cases, participate in client consultations, learn how lawyers get paid, attend court hearings, etc. Whether you get to experience all of those will vary, depending on where you choose to intern. It is best to ask those questions during the interview so that you do not choose a firm where all you do is research. Having good research skills is important, but it gets boring quickly. You should look for a mixture of assignments.

When I interned at the District Attorney's office, I asked my supervisor to split up my Fridays. Half of my Friday I completed in-office assignments, and the other half I spent in court. I found this invaluable. Anyone can attend court hearings. You do not have to intern at the local prosecutor's office to do so. Do it now. Do it before you start law school. They post the schedules in the courtroom. You can sit in on anything from arraignments to jury selection to summations in a murder trial. I sat in all of those and more, even a full manslaughter trial. I always wanted to be a litigator, so I found the courtroom really interesting.

<u>Side note</u>: If you want to be a courtroom lawyer— a litigator, go into criminal law.

Civil cases rarely go to trial. Most of them are settled out of court, and lawyers seldom have to get in front of a judge. Civil litigation is just a heavy motion practice. It can get boring depending on the law you practice and your interests. Perhaps I was naïve, but I did not realize this until I interned at the small firms and the District Attorney's office. It was a night and day difference. Of course, you will make less money working for the government, but the experience will last a lifetime. Even if you did not get that dream corporate job out of law school, big firms love to recruit former prosecutors. They know you are trained well in trial advocacy, research, and writing skills, and have a tremendous work ethic. Another benefit is loan forgiveness.

The government forgives loans after ten years for lawyers working in public interest. During those ten years, you pay a small percentage of your salary towards the student loans. In my opinion, the experience is worth it even if you do it for a few years.

# 8

# WIN

*Always Put Yourself in a Position to Win
by Embracing the Hard Work.*

For me, it was worth putting in those seventy to eight hours per week into work, school, and internships. After my second year, I was invited to various On Campus Interviews (OCIs). If you are a full time student, you will do this after your first year. OCI is a program where the top firms come to your law school to recruit top candidates. I am by no means a top candidate in terms of grades. They are a predominately a mixture of B's and B+'s with some A's and A-'s. Most recruiting firms are looking for students in the top 10–20% of the class and with some Law Review, Journal, or Moot Court experience. Some firms will not even accept resumes from those who do not have that experience because interview slots are limited. One firm may only interview ten to fifteen candidates, but only offer one position to a candidate. Have I mentioned law school is ultra-competitive?

During OCI, you will interview to get into the firms' Summer Associate programs for the following summer. The best part is that these positions are paid. Top law firms pay their Summer Associates at the same level as first-year Associates (annual compensation is prorated for eight to ten weeks depending on the length of the summer program). Compensation varies firm to firm, but is currently about $150,000/year on the low end and as high as $200,000/year at the very elite firms. Full-time offers are made at the end of the summer program, and, if you accept, you return to the firm after graduation.

Remember, in the previous chapter I noted why it is so important for you to crush your first year classes (and second year for part-time students)? I also said to get on Law Review or a journal and/or get on the moot court team. This is why. For part-time students working full-time, it is more realistic to get on only one of those. Just do it. It is worth it for the OCI. I do not want to give the impression that it is only the very elite firms that come to the OCI – they do, but there are other prestigious organizations that also come to interview. This includes the local prosecutor's office, legal aid society, the city's law department, the US military's Judge Advocate General (JAG), and many more. Most students want to and should participate in OCI.

If you want that high paying corporate job, you should apply to every single firm that matches with your credentials. If you are not on Law Review, a journal, or part of the moot court, apply to those that "prefer," but do not "require" that participation. Prefer is a nice way of saying that they will take the students who do have the relevant experience before they even look at you. One other thing that all the firms will require—your resume. I knew my resume was a killer. Because of my full-time work experience and internships, I was confident that at least some firms would give me an opportunity for an interview. What did I have to lose? Nothing. Neither will you. Just apply. They will either invite you or they will not. Once they do invite you, bring your A game to the interview.

That is exactly what I did. I applied to every single firm and organization I possibly could. I was even invited for interviews with the prosecutor's office, the NYC Law Department, and JAG. Since these interviews were for positions the following summer, I wanted to have as many options as possible. Do not limit yourself. I landed a few interviews and then a few offers. At every interview I was asked, "Why law school?" Remember, they will ask you this no matter what, especially for part-time students who are looking for a career change or career progression. The interviewers were even more curious about my job and internships and how I did it all simultaneously. Remember, talent matters. Most candidates at OCI were more talented than I was when you compared the transcripts. Employers undoubtedly value talent, but they also value those who work hard. And when you compared resumes, my hard work beat my talent. In the end, I accepted an offer to be a summer associate at a corporate law firm for this upcoming summer. If you are wondering how I am going to manage that with work, the answer is I am not going to. I will be taking a leave of absence from my regular job for the summer.

I worked very hard and prepared all of law school to be in this position. For this I am grateful. However, as I have mentioned, not everyone will land an OCI position. That is perfectly fine. You have an alternative. You should browse your law school career services websites where they post internships, jobs, and other opportunities. Many well-known mid-size firms do not participate in OCI, but they post positions via law school career services. At my law school, banks like JP Morgan Chase and Goldman Sachs always post positions for their tax, compliance, legal, and trust departments. If that is something you are interested in, then apply. Just keep applying to anything and everything that piques your interest. This is also the alternative for those who cannot do or repeat semester-long internships because you should spend a summer working somewhere. Try to take a leave from your current job or, if you are looking to change careers, quit if you can.

You do not want to be in a position after law school where you learn that practicing law is so much different than learning the law. Now you have wasted all this money and time preparing for a career you do not enjoy. Why not go through this process while you are in school? At least you may learn about an area of law you definitely do not want to be in. It is much harder to become a trial lawyer after being a corporate lawyer than it is to become a trial lawyer after taking a bunch of corporate law classes in law school. Internships and summer positions are essentially a risk free way of getting your feet wet. You are not confined to that area of law for life. Best-case scenario, you find what you really like, and one of the places where you intern may invite you to come back full-time after you graduate.

The firm where I am interning right now has just hired an associate who was their spring intern last year.

This experience will only benefit you and make you stand out as a candidate. I cannot stress the importance of this enough. You do not want to graduate and then figure it all out. I have several friends in law school who do not take advantage of this. I ask them, "Did you apply anywhere through OCI, attend this networking event, take more than the one required internship or clinic, or do you know where you will be working when you graduate in two months?" They do not have a clue as to what they will be doing. Heck, a few do not even know how to properly structure their legal resume. Do this all while in law school. I tell them what I have been doing, and they look at me like I am crazy. If desiring to be meaningfully employed is crazy, then I hope I am the craziest person in law school.

I approach this as if I do not have a job to fall back to. I do – I am still a police officer, remember? I still took on more internships after the OCI offer because I am going through law school like I have everything to lose. You have to be in it with the same mentality. Be all in. You do not want to end up like several of my friends. How they spend all this time and money without a clue as to where they plan to be after graduation is beyond me. I do not want you to end up like them. YOU do not want to end up like them.

The friends I speak of are going to find some job doing document review and blame their law schools for not getting them their dream job making a six-figure salary. Even if you have rich lawyer friends or you come from a family of attorneys, you should conduct your business as if they do not exist. Remember, always put yourself in a position to win. I have friends who coasted through law school because they said they were just going to work for their fathers or in the family business afterwards. For some, it has worked out that way just fine. For others, it has not. Now they are in shock to find out that most places that want to hire them will start them at $50,000 per year with no benefits. This is when the regret of going to law school begins to set it in. It is not law school that let you down. It is you who let you down.

Law school is not like medical or dental school. You are not practically guaranteed a job and six figure salary long-term. Medicine is a field always high in demand. So is law, but it can be cyclical, and different practices thrive at different times. You have to constantly hustle if you want to be a successful lawyer. I bring this up again because you should never go to law school for just money. You are going to learn the hard way there are way more lawyers making $60,000 than $600,000. I know both of these lawyers. Guess who of them hustled? Even public interest attorneys hustle. Most of them believe the cause they are a part of. They do it with a purpose. And I will say it again. If you did not begin law school with the proper purpose, odds are you will be unhappy.

I do not want to sound like I am against you changing careers once you are already a lawyer. What I *am* trying to do is save you the aggravation of experiencing it. Like I said, I see it every day in friends who are students and friends who are seasoned lawyers. They hate it. Some of this aggravation can be saved in law school by focusing on your goals and taking appropriate steps towards them. Do not worry about what you are going to wear at Barrister's Ball in spring. Worry about how you can improve your grades, what area of the law interests you, cross out what you definitely do not want to do, and take advantage of your time in law school. Parties like Barrister's Ball will always be there. Side note: I have yet to attend one and at this rate I probably will not get to it. You may choose to, however. From what I hear, it is a great time.

# 9

# MAKE LAW SCHOOL COUNT

*Skills pay bills*

If you have decided to attend law school after reading this short book, Bravo! I am extremely happy for you. Each chapter is written to set you up for success. I have not written anything in this book that is controversial or severely debatable. As you can tell by the price of this book, I did not do it to become rich. I wrote this book because I want you to be in a position to win before you even begin your journey. I did not go into excessive details about each year in law school because you have probably heard many stories from other people. How you are going to brief a case is not important at this time. What is important is that you know what you are getting yourself into. If you are doing it without a purpose, it is not worth it. If you are doing it for just money, you will not enjoy it. Plenty of other things to do out there for just money.

What I do want from you is to keep this book around during your time in school. The core principles in the book will never change. You will always have to work hard and hustle. If you do, you will enjoy your time in law school. You will also enjoy your career as an attorney. There is something special when a client comes into your office with a problem, and you can help find a solution for them. It reminds me of when I was an officer on patrol working midnights in Bedstuy. Someone calls 911, and you get to be there to help them. I have my reasons for not continuing that and transitioning into this part of the legal profession, but the concept to me is no different. I want to be in it to solve problems. It does not matter if it is for a single mother who is losing her house due to a foreclosure, or for a billion-dollar corporation, which alleges that their intellectual property has been illegally compromised. There is something special about this profession.

So, again, go into it with a sense of purpose. Follow the core advice in this book. It is there to help you. There are other books out there that will teach you how to take law school exams or how to network in law school, but they are not going to give you some of the tools that I am providing in this concise manner. I am not going to sit here and tell you that if you do everything in this book, you will get your dream job. Some factors out of your control can prevent that. But if you do decide to follow the core principles in this book, you will put yourself in a position to win as I have. I do not know how my summer at the big firm will turn out. I also do not know how my career as an attorney will develop. What I do know is that I will always hustle and do my best to be in a position to win. I have made a commitment, and you should do as well if you decide to go through and finish law school.

As I have repeatedly said, law school is a commitment of your time and money. Even if you are going for free, you have to take the opportunity costs into account. Therefore, you must make law school count. You will have fun, you will make life-long relationships or even partnerships; you will be tested intellectually like you have never been tested before; and most importantly, you can and you will get through it successfully. It is an investment in you. It will last a lifetime. Make it count!

> *"Generally speaking, investing in yourself is the best thing you can do. Anything that improves your own talents; nobody can tax it or take it away from you. They can run up huge deficits and the dollar can become worth far less. You can have all kinds of things happen. But if you've got talent yourself, and you've maximized your talent, you've got a tremendous asset that can return ten-fold."* - Warren Buffet

www.ingramcontent.com/pod-product-compliance
Lightning Source LLC
Chambersburg PA
CBHW061233180526
45170CB00003B/1270